THIS BOOK BELONGS TO:

___

Made in the USA
Monee, IL
15 October 2021

80116812R00065